'95

Christmas 2001

love Amy &
BREW
x x x

# the book of life's firsts

by luke de saintonge

and illustrated by jim lefevre

**Nightingale Press**

*an imprint of Wimbledon Publishing Company Ltd.*

LONDON

Copyright © 2001
Illustrations © 2001 WPC

First published in Great Britain
by Wimbledon Publishing Co. Ltd.
London  P.O. Box 9779  SW19 7ZG

ISBN: 1903222 29 X

Produced in Great Britain
Printed and bound in Hungary

With special thanks for their contributions and insight:


David Chaput de Saintonge
Rebecca Chaput de Saintonge
Sally Franz
Mikki Goffin
Dan Gorlov
Noel McPherson
Stuart Ryan

# INTRODUCTION

I remember my first day at school: that curious mixture of independence and apprehension that rapidly became terror as Mum waved goodbye. And that first fight: knees quaking, mercifully over in seconds, but leaving the realization that life can hit back hard. And then that first, fumbled kiss: anticipated for so long and ultimately clumsy, yet completely euphoric. Here, as with all of life's firsts, I was grappling with unfamiliar territory and enjoying what I found.

These first experiences shaped who I am, and will continue to do so. In reading this book I found myself time and time again, sometimes with a smile, sometimes with sadness and often with a wistful sense of recollection. Overall, in these pages you will recognize yourself, as you were, as you are and how you will become, regardless of age or background. If you are young, see what life has in store; if you are old read on and reminisce; if, like me, you find yourself somewhere in the middle, look forward to the first day of retirement whilst trying to forget that first grey hair.

This is a book crafted by writers and artists who have loved, laughed and been moved by life. All come from different backgrounds and ages, but have ultimately faced life's firsts and live to tell the tale.

Stuart Ryan 2001

# the first tooth

For a brief time, a baby represents the pure, unspoiled essence of humanity: smooth, soft, fragile and innocent, the newborn infant is the image of its parents, stripped of every harsh and uncomfortable edge. Its perfection is mesmerizing.

Then, one night, the wails and screams become just that little harsher and more uncomfortable than before: the child begins to teethe. Now family enchantment becomes mingled with uncertainty - as fate bestows one defiant buck-tooth on its child, who now possesses a small weapon with which it can learn to draw blood. For nervous mothers, the first tooth often encourages the purchase of the first milk bottle.

# first word

Few remember their first word. Most are later guided through this milestone by nostalgic relatives who thought they caught it. But their reminiscence should be treated with caution. It's easy to decipher simple babble when noone's really got a clue what it means. All babies are considered 'gurglers' until the day a creative ear catches half a syllable of the word 'Mummy' amidst the gobbledy-gook. *Then* they are deemed 'talkers'.

Some child psychologists share a different view: that babies know exactly what they're saying long before a doting mother decides to translate liberally out of baby-speak. But I guess this proposes a rather difficult scenario for loving, self-respecting parents. Which woman wants to hear her child call out 'mamamama' knowing it is not a first declaration of love, but an attempt at the phrase "Mother - how long *are* you going to make me sit in my own sewage?"

3

# the first birthday

Theoretically this anniversary should be the cheapest of celebrations - the birthday baby has no friends yet, no desire for ice cream and jelly, no logical comprehension of magicians, clowns, party games, balloons or streamers. It will almost certainly have no memory of the event in later life. And, to top it all, one needs only a single candle for the token birthday cupcake.

But it never works out like this. As if the increasing burden of overpriced baby gear is not enough, new parents feel compelled to celebrate the first birthday with gusto, if only for their own benefit. As a one-year-old, therefore, you will likely see in your first year lying on your back, staring at the faces of simpering wrinklies in colourful party hats, watching them eat and drink and exchange birthday cards on your behalf. Wet kiss after wet kiss will give you your first sniff of wine and cheap perfume. Long rounds of 'hug the baby' for every member of the extended family will give you an early distaste for Graeco-Roman wrestling.

Is it all worth the new rattle? Thirteen years later, when Mum shows your first date the birthday photos, I guess you'll know for sure.

# the first toy

A child's first toys are designed to have some kind of positive effect on its life. Building blocks improve hand-eye coordination and creativity; a baby's rattle provides a gentle workout; colourful, squishy, squeaky things encourage an early understanding that farts are funny. But, arguably more important than any of these is the ubiquitous cuddly animal.

The first toy is almost always some fluffy little creature, left by parents in a baby's cot. Their reasoning must be that such a companion will help found their child's empathy and love for creation. This seems to work most of the time. Prolonged childhood obsessions with dolphins, horses, pigs, lobsters, gibbons and giraffe are all commonplace - no doubt a positive result of having shared a pillow with a stuffed likeness for years.

Unfortunately, as anyone who remembers *Gremlins* will know, there can be a fine line between cute and macabre. So pity the poor child who suffers for his parents poor judgement and lack of taste, who fades meekly into the corners of classrooms and stares night after night into the empty grin of the *Poltergeist* clown.

Most kids want to be vets or marine biologists when they grow up, but there's always one, still haunted by the Satanic glint in Teddy's eyes that dreams of taxidermy or pathology.

# the first steps

You have been crawling excitedly around for several months before your parents really decide to put your legs to the test. You only have yourself to blame. Prior to this, whenever Daddy held you upright for a bit of nappy sniffing you had taken the opportunity to thrash yourself around like a fish out of water. How else should a parent respond when their fourteen-month-old performs such a startling impersonation of Linford Christie after a bottle of whiskey?

So there you are, in the hallway, Mum behind, her grasp on your waist weakening, Dad, a couple of metres in front, arms outspread, his face set with encouragement and concentration. Suddenly a push, a thrash of the legs, a brief, sublime moment of self-propulsion - then panic, disorientation and a hard, cold wall hits the side of your head.

"Whoops-a-daisy!" - Mother, smiling.

"Now that wasn't too hard, was it?" - Father, beaming.

("I think I swallowed my tongue," - you, eating the carpet.)

# the first sibling

Children are ruthless creatures. And who can blame them? They spend the first two-and-a-half years crawling around, cooing and dribbling - frustrated that no one can understand them. Then, when they've finally begun to learn all those valuable words, so useful when wanting your bottom wiped *immediately*, Mother goes and produces another baby.

You're two-and-a-half and back at square one - you've learnt how to get what you want, but no one's listening any more. Mother's too busy cleaning, feeding and winding her new arrival to look after you, and Father's never there, working overtime to pay for the extra nappies. The whole situation is infuriating. They'd just taught you how to walk, talk and use a potty. There was no need for them to go through it again.

There is, however, a positive side to this whole sham: You look at your old *Action Man* with a dent in his head, one leg and both arms missing, then you turn to your new sister, still perfectly intact, asleep in her cot. You realize you may have found a new toy.

# the first lie

Adults often tell their kids, "Honesty is the best policy". Note the choice of words - not 'most virtuous policy' or 'most moral' - just 'best'. This rather vague maxim seems to imply it's just safer to be honest. Dishonesty, as the adults know, is damned hard to get away with.

Kids, however, have little idea how hard it is to pull off a good lie. Sure enough, in defiance of their parents' advice, it's not long before they launch themselves cluelessly into the most outrageous whoppers. The first lie is always the best - so ill-conceived and transparent, it is more hilarious than harmful. The toddler with honey in his eyes, up his nose and dripping from his hair will always deny he has been in the jar. He is, as yet, unaware of the simple logic of incriminating evidence. He will soon learn to frame his sister.

Perhaps it is empathy that makes his mother laugh this time. It was, after all, just the other night that his father came home late from 'squash' with beer breath and a packet of pork scratchings hanging out of the back of his suit.

# the first friend

The adult world tends to mould people into very self-sufficient and isolated individuals. From early on, our awareness of people's physical and intellectual differences encourages rivalry, fragmentation and cliquism. After adolescence, most of us seem ready to go it alone, aware of what makes us conspicuous or peculiar, and keen to lead our lives either disguising or nurturing these traits.

We wind up far from the innocent days of childhood - days when friends were made with a single word or glance. Hence the enchantment with which adults watch youngsters play: the toddler in the sandpit, making friends by offering the nearest child a piece of the hardened animal poo he has unearthed. A strange, but genuinely altruistic gesture, from a period in life when friendships are based on proximity more than anything else. An exchange, a sniff, a curious gaze into new eyes and a bond is forged. A precious link in a fragmented world.

The two continue to dig quietly, as yet unaware of the awkwardness of silence or the impropriety of exchanging excrement. But, through all the increasing pressures of growing up, it remains the purest act of friendship.

# first day at school

So much emphasis is put on the first day at school it seems many kids go believing that 'school' is, in fact, a one-day phenomenon - like a trip to the zoo. For the innocent five-year-old boy it must seem like some kind of fancy dress party, his parents preparing him with blazer, grey shorts, stripy tie, felt cap and leather satchel, taking photos and talking about 'new friends'.

Hence the bravery of the youngest pupils on their first day, who return from their brief foray into the world of education believing themselves to have just a few more days tutelage ahead of them - one called 'college', another called 'University'. A short conversation with Father is sufficient for the young boy to understand that he has another two hundred lessons of 'Show and Tell' before the year is even out, and if he can imagine studying increasingly hard for the entire first third of his life, he might have a better idea of what's expected of him.

The next day, screaming youngsters have to be crow-barred out of their parent's cars and brought kicking and screaming into the classroom. They now know that from here on in fun is *earnt*. And it'll be six hours hard graft with the crayons before they can go home and destroy the living room again.

# the first pet

There comes a time when your fluffy toy pig - affectionately known as 'Pig' - loses his appeal. His squeaky buttocks were hilarious the first few thousand times you squeezed them, but you're older now and your demands on the world are more sophisticated. Pig lies dejected for several months before your parents realize you're getting bored of your inanimate friends.

Then, one day, you are presented with a small cardboard box. Inside, nestled into layers of straw and tissue paper you find a new playmate - your first pet.

Fortunes split here, depending on the creature found within. We learn much about life and love from our first pets: kids who are knocked down every day by an over-enthusiastic Rottweiler stand a better chance of growing into passionate and resilient individuals. Those who have to check every hour that their hamster hasn't arrested on the tread-wheel risk living nervous lives, forever checking behind them for murderers or 'kick me' signs. And those who simply have to make do with the company of 'Pig', will only ever feel at home when breaking wind or watching Benny Hill videos. All of which is nothing compared to the child who keeps tropical fish and is destined to grieve every time he enters a lavatory.

# the first fight

Gradually, sand-pit sessions give way to *Action Man* and innocent exchanges of dog poo are no longer the staple for close friendships. Such gestures are replaced by machine gun sound effects and epic re-enactions of Combat Joe taking on the Korean army. Harmony becomes competition as you vie with your friends for the biggest, baddest superhero toy with the most lethal photon-blaster. In short, you learn to oppose one another.

Before long, Combat Joe is decapitated, half of Korea has been levelled by aliens and you are outside with a football. Indirect conflict has had its day, and you have graduated to contact sports. This is when you first notice that the geeky rich kid who had the best toys can't actually run properly, whilst some of your other friends are considerably faster and stronger than you. Battle is much harder when you can't rely on Combat Joe. Worse still for the geeky rich kid.

Down by 10-2 and bruised by the big boys, you get a taste of the inequalities and injustices which, sure enough, will pepper the rest of your life. It's only when big Tom Flannigan steals your mate's football that you decide to take a stand - unarmed and uninitiated, alone against injustice.

Some minutes later, as you pick your bloodied face out of the mud, you begin to understand that, in the real world, people pick their battles.

# first make-up

It starts with the high heels - the disgusting patent leather red stilettos you find in the bottom of your mum's wardrobe. You parade in front of the mirror, feeling tall and important (but looking absurd). After hobbling around, you progress onto a few other select items from her wardrobe - a chiffon headscarf perhaps, a floral wrap-around skirt, or maybe just an old net curtain draped over your head. Then you find yourself drawn to the cosmetics bag on the dressing table, which spills over with blusher compacts, powdery brushes, a rainbow of lipsticks and eyeshadows, squeezy tubes of skin-coloured goo, wands of mascara in every shade. What does this strange paddle-type thing do, you wonder. You dip it in a pot of bronzing pearls and swish it over your face. A quick mirror check confirms you look great. How about a bit of eyeshadow? Lagoon blue or mermaid green? How about both? On it goes - the eyelids, under the eyes and a bit on the cheeks maybe. Mascara - loads of it. Big black clumpy lashes, like a collection of squashed spider legs. Blusher in flamingo pink on the cheeks. And the forehead - it's feeling left out. So is your chin, actually. Daub it with a more subtle shade - bubblegum cerise.

Then you notice your mum, behind you, cross-armed and frowning - not exactly delighted by this exciting new appearance? She angrily tidies up her make-up bag and orders you to your room to think about how ridiculous you're being. You slink away guiltily.

Of course, if you're a girl your mum's reaction may not be quite so stern.

# First Spot

The dawning of your sexual identity coincides cruelly with the eruption of acne. In an ironic travesty of justice, the same hormones that render you desperate to attract a mate also make you look like a freshly baked pizza. A lucky few may breeze through their teens without a single blemish, but for most, the horror of a facial breakout is a very real and regular threat.

Even if you are not cursed with full-on widespread acne, the odd boil is almost certain to crop up. All too often this is on the eve of a first date or some other important event. You will agonise over your oily, pock-marked skin in the mirror only to be told by your parents 'Don't squeeze! It will only make them worse.' Worse? How could it be any worse? Your face scares young children. Dammit, it scares you. Never has the word 'pimple' seemed so inadequate when referring to the volcanic carbuncle on the end of your nose. How can you be taken seriously when you look like an uncensored 'before' picture in a Clearasil ad? How can you 'get lucky' when Mount Etna is primed to explode on your extremities?

Your peers complain about their spots as well, but you're convinced yours are the most obvious, unsightly and tenacious. Various potions and lotions will be slapped onto the offending areas with liberal abandon in the hope that your face will revert back to the peaches-and-cream complexion you once had. But their effect is minimal. Unfortunately, spots are just another of puberty's many trials - along with wet dreams, excess body hair, gusset stains and penis/breast-size angst. They simply have to be tolerated until you finally blossom into a beautifully spot-free, well-adjusted adult ... some six or seven years later.

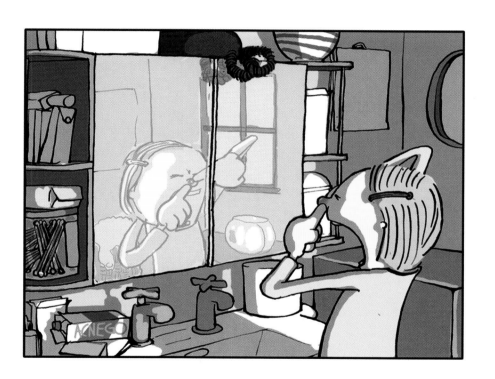

# the first pube

Pubic hair is a funny thing - perhaps the most obvious sign that maturity is on its way. At ten some of your friends probably had them tucked secretly away whilst you were building lego battle-stations. Others may see no more than the softest down the wrong side of twenty.

In the changing rooms at junior school there was always the big kid who kept his swimming shorts on all the time because he didn't want anyone to see what appeared to be a squirrel hibernating in his trunks. As you get older the sense of embarrassment reverses. Soon it is the big kid who spends half an hour butt-naked in the shower, boldly soaping his hirsute appendage, whilst you remain imprisoned in your Speedo's. Now you guard your darkest secret desperately: that manhood has not called for you; you have been overlooked; Mother Nature has neglected to water your acorn.

The first pube is therefore a difficult thing to spot. Either you look down at ten and jump at the bushy tangle clinging to your groin, or you scrutinize each blonde hair through a magnifying glass at fifteen to see if you can spot a dark one. Either way they just seem to creep up on you - preceded or precipitated by the utter humiliation that only adolescence can bring.

# First Period

As a curious child, who could forget the strange little boxes in Mummy's bottom drawer, filled with cotton wool mice in cellophane? What were they for? What did the string do? Why did they go all big and weird when you dunked them in water?

Gradually you learn that something pretty extraordinary is about to happen to you. You inspect the clean crotches of innocent panties daily and the slightest bellyache conveys great hope that, at last, the time has arrived.

Then one day, you wake to find your pyjamas magnificently sullied. Your patience is rewarded in a starburst of vivid crimson, displaying the blindingly obvious: you are physically able to have babies.

Welcome to five days of grouchiness, pain and mess every month for the next thirty years of your life. You find out why Claire Rayner got so excited about 'wings'. You finally discover what to do with those little mice during an emotional 'tampon ceremony' conducted by a slightly flustered mother. Male members of the family sink into polite, mortified silence as you and your mother rejoice in this momentous breakthrough. You are a 'fully functional female'.

Unfortunately, once you've got over the thrill of your first, the lesser thrill of your second, the relative misery of your third and the hundreds that follow, you come to see this wondrous symbol of Womanhood for what it really is: a monthly bloody pain.

# first bra

Of course you don't need it, but that's not the point. By the ripe old age of ten or eleven you have already spent entire evenings in front of the mirror puffing out your chest and convincing yourself that your slightly enlarged nipples constitute a bosom that *must* be supported. You need, as a matter of urgency, an 'over the shoulder boulder holder'.

This is your first foray into the rituals of femininity, of adulthood. No longer is 'AA' merely a size of battery - something you realise as an over-zealous shop assistant ties her tape measure around your rib cage and utters the words "You're a 98AA". You feel you've died and gone to Heaven. You have a *size!* Your mother resists the urge to snigger, and buys the miniscule scrap of decorated cotton.

As a garment, it is perfectly functionless and quite absurd, but you will not know this until you find it discarded ten years later at the back of your wardrobe. To you, at this euphoric moment, it is wonderful - beautifully adorned with rosebuds and bows. You intend to wear it every day for the rest of your life...or at least until you require a size upgrade.

Of course, this is before you have spent hours in your room contorting yourself into strange positions trying in vain to fasten it. And then spent even longer attempting to get the damned thing off. Before the telltale outline has provoked the boys at school to creep up on you from behind and ping your straps. Before it has left red indents on your back and shoulders. And before you have gone back to your room, prayed your breasts don't get any bigger, thrown your bra into the back of your wardrobe and put on one of your sensible vests instead.

# first date

Hormones do weird things to you, never more so than during adolescence when your smooth, pink body is transformed into a greasy, hairy mass of spots and newly-sprouted appendages. What's more, they complicate your thought processes and give you strange urges, so that basic speech and sensory-motor skills suddenly become those of a blundering, jabbering gibbon.

The opposite sex - once shunned and avoided - are now viewed as objects of wonder; mysterious creatures with different appendages but, more importantly, the same urges. Teenage boys may find their brains turn to mush when attempting to converse with a girl (while their uncontrollable protuberance may do the exact opposite) - all part of the embarrassment of growing up. But it's only when you are forced into terrifyingly intimate encounters (otherwise known as 'dates') that the real fun begins.

You may only be thirteen years old, but romance is not a totally alien concept. Boys know that girls like flowers, soppy films starring Meg Ryan, candlelit dinners, good manners and respect. Girls know that boys want something altogether different. First dates provide the ideal occasion for young girls and boys to get to grips with these gross sexual misalignments.

Many is the young lad who discovers painfully that a bag of chips, a lewd joke and a can of ginger beer does not earn him the right to grope the girl next to him. And many is the young lady who finds out that, just because she's been asked out, doesn't mean she'll be dining at five star restaurants or going to the ballet. Hence lengthy silences in and around cinemas, where dates needn't look at each other and can keep popcorn in their mouths to avoid the embarrassment of conversation.

# First girlfriend or boyfriend

The last time you had a girlfriend or boyfriend didn't really count: on the playground at six years old you could pick someone at random - it wasn't necessary to check with them first. A friend would quiz you, "Who's your girlfriend?" and that would be your cue to choose, "Errrrm...Sharon". The great thing was you didn't really have to talk to Sharon once she was yours. You could carry on playing 'kiss chase' and just make sure you caught her a few more times than normal. There was something reassuring about having a 'special someone', even if mutual contact was minimal.

Now things are different, girls have curves, wear make-up and tight clothes, their mere presence makes you feel giddy and, on top of all of this, they expect you to talk to them. Securing that 'special someone' becomes just as necessary, but infinitely more difficult. Not least because your lips quiver and you lose the sensation in your legs whenever you try to make small talk with one of these sirens.

Finally you hazard into a conversation with a young girl who doesn't seem put off as you twitch nervously before her. You realize you'd better seize the opportunity whilst she's there and ask her to McDonald's at the weekend. She says, "okay". And that's it! Your first proper girlfriend. The rest is just holding hands, walking around shopping arcades and occasionally having conversations about homework - but that's not really important. What's important is that you've broken into the world of adult relationships and acquainted yourself with 'women'. This means that when you get bored of each other in a week's time, you can exchange her for one of her mates and set her up with one of yours.

# FIRST KISS

You have practised on posters of film and pop idols, on the back of your hand, on your pillow, perhaps even on the family pet if you were ever feeling particularly frisky. It wasn't long ago that the thought of touching tongues with someone else was repugnant to you, but now you're desperate to try it. All your friends have.

So you prepare yourself for the year nine disco, expecting the first kiss to send you reeling into starry-eyed rapture. Expecting to melt into the romantic embrace of a French-kissing expert with minty fresh breath and nice teeth. NOT expecting to be grabbed roughly during 'Agadoo' and pushed up against the wall for a session of sink-plunger face-sucking, nor to be left with the aftertaste of his chili sauce cheeseburger supper in your mouth.

A good kiss requires a fair amount of practice and the first kiss is invariably an awkward affair, particularly if your partner has braces: a clashing of teeth, a tongue up a nostril, a bit of dribble and a lot of hot, clumsy breathing. Funnily enough, this is something teenagers don't mind working hard to perfect. They can spend days on end inside strange mouths, exploring the terrain. Worried parents have been known to feed their children intravenously during this dangerous 'limpet stage'.

# the first job

Parents never seem to understand the growing financial needs of their children. At nine, it was thirty pence a week for a chocolate bar. Now you're a teenager, they've barely kept up with inflation, let alone the increasing need for Playstation software. Your father's advice doesn't really help ("In my day, a lad like you would be sweeping chimneys"). So you're left with one option - get a job.

But what a glorious occasion this proves to be for a young boy or girl. The financial freedom that comes with social responsibility! Up with the sun and out on the bike, delivering the news to bleary-eyed townsfolk. Or coffees and teas in cafes for shoppers in need of refreshment all hand-brewed by you. Then weekends on checkouts in markets and food halls, ensuring that larders and fridges stay stocked.

This is the life beyond your doorstep. A life in which you can play a part. A life that rewards your experiences of freedom with a wage by the hour and a sense of fulfillment. Sure, it can be tough, and lonely sometimes, but when you're out there and earning - just you against the world - it's easy to remember why you're doing it...

# first time drunk

Attitudes to alcohol vary according to exposure. Those with parents who drink may well have been offered the odd glass, perhaps spent giddy moments as an eleven-year-old tottering around a family wedding reception, maybe even an emergency stomach pump after stumbling across the drinks cabinet and polishing off their mother's apricot brandy. Those with more sober parents will be content drinking lemon squash until tales of cider-drinking begin to infiltrate the classroom. Then they learn of a different type of refreshment: "You drank how many gallons? ...You ended up *where* naked?"

By fifteen or sixteen these disparate attitudes tend to have levelled out. At this stage most adolescents are united in a common desire to obliterate their senses with intoxicants and stage carefully unsupervised 'parties', where one can experiment with liquor. Here teenagers revel in their first experiences of freedom and escapism ... for about forty minutes at least, until they polish off their six pack of export lager and pass out in a warm pool of their own vomit.

But this doesn't deter the young revelers. It's many years before they learn to use phrases like 'that's my limit' or 'just a lemonade, please'. In the meantime, they take it in turns to poison themselves, lock themselves in toilets and wake up in casualty. As for those that don't take part, well, their time comes sooner or later. And office parties wouldn't be the same without them.

# first major exam

**M**ajor exams are amongst the most daunting of life's milestones: Some 'first times' can be conveniently forgotten, the first exam cannot. Whatever happens, your performance stays with you, represented by a small grade or number which is forever associated with your name. That's quite serious.

Hence, come April and May, young scholars suddenly grow out of cider and chunder, begin rushing to and fro with files and start inhabiting strange places like libraries. Boys now compare revision hours done per day as opposed to pints drunk per weekend. Girls now compare elegant notes as opposed to fashionable outfits and, for a time, adolescence becomes a very serious place indeed.

Unfortunately, it rarely matters how many hours are done before the big day. In this kind of make-or-break situation it all comes down to nerve. For many, conscientiousness and focus have given way to blind panic by the time they enter the examination room. Inevitably, minds go blank.

It's only after the exam that candidates find they were not alone in their agony and that many others had problems with the first question: "Yes I knew the second part was Witherspoon, but I couldn't for the life of me remember my *first* name".

# first beard

One day you wake up and it all just seems to make sense. All those years of awkwardness and shame as you wrestled with the problems of growing up suddenly seem well spent. You think about your life now: you've got a picture of a girl in your wallet, you're taller than your Dad and can get away with swearing at your Mum, you get into pubs without being asked for ID, drink more than your big brother, can blow smoke rings, grow hairs on your chest, win arm wrestles, break hearts. It's all there - all the ingredients which make the man ... apart from perhaps one thing.

You get out of bed and step over piles of worn and soiled underwear to reach the mirror. In the early morning light, you examine the growth you have been nurturing for a week and immediately crack a knowing grin. Yes! It's there! There at last! A beard! Not down, not wisps, not stubble - but surely now just the right amount of bushy coverage to merit the title of 'beard'. You kind of knew it was going to be ready today. It just felt right. You again admire the reflection in the mirror, now suddenly complete, and realize with startling clarity, 'I am a man'. Who'd have thought that the transition from boyhood would be so obvious. So clear-cut? So conspicuous? As you head down for breakfast, you exaggerate your characteristic swagger, just so Mum and Dad know: you've arrived!

# first holiday without parents

Years of being forced into month-long family holidays in Guernsey have not had the effect your parents would have wanted. Far from developing a respect and admiration for turn-of-the-century stately homes, sun-bathing in fourteen degrees on stony beaches and anagram games in the back of the car, you feel unfulfilled by your trips into the big, wide world.

Twelve months later you are standing in your backpack, with your two best mates waving goodbye to your parents at Portsmouth. "Be sensible!" they advise, "If you get into trouble, call us! No matter where you are." As if! you think, tearing into duty-frees on the ferry, eager to make the most of your new freedom. An hour later you're drinking beer, smoking fags at the bar and winking at the girls in the Dutch tour party on the other side of the ferry. By four o'clock you're mildly wasted on top deck and emptying your guts into the English Channel below. Coming in to dock at Saint Malo, and you're patting your pockets in panic, trying to explain to your friends what's happened to the wallets you were supposed to look after. Before long you're all stranded without francs on a foreign roadside, hoping you'll be able to find a youth hostel that accepts discount aftershave in exchange for rooms. At eight pm that night you're ringing home to convince your father to wire some money into your account. By eleven, sleeping in a doorway in Rennes, you secretly wish you'd stayed with Mum and Dad on the Isle of Wight.

And so it goes on. You all survive, of course. Travel is all about survival. You just don't do it on topless beaches and fancy Riviera bars, as you'd planned. Luckily, your fraternal pact of secrecy ensures that the holiday woes remain unspoken. And, as far as the rest of your classmates are concerned, your holiday in Greece with the Swedish national netball team was a blast.

# first contraception

**Y**ou are on the brink of your first sexual relationship. The flirting, teasing and courting are all coming to a head and you are looking at the distinct possibility of securing for yourself a 'partner'. This means several things: massive phone bills, less nights out with your mates, more nights in with Meg Ryan videos. But, more important than all of these: sex on tap.

Typically, girls and boys make different preparations for this eventuality. Worried about pregnancy, health, hygiene and the emotional effects of sexual relations, many girls will want to discuss the pros and cons of the situation at the local family planning clinic. Any decision to take the contraceptive pill is made only with a thorough evaluation of its safety, efficiency and side-effects.

Boys on the other hand, worried about having to say the word 'condom' out loud in the chemists, take their problems with them, as ever, to the pub. Here our would-be Casanova keeps a few pound coins back from his first round and disappears into the toilets. Any decision to buy condoms is made with a thorough evaluation of whether his partner prefers banana to strawberry, ribs to bumps or red to glow-in-the-dark green. Then its back out to the bar to show the lads the new acquisition: One *King-Kong Twin Turret Invader* - for 'guaranteed pleasure'. Minimum embarrassment, maximum fun - that's what sex is all about isn't it? Well, yes, until he finds it fits like a verruca sock on a frankfurter.

# first sex

Sexual maturity reaches its climactic (or, indeed, non-climactic) *dénouement* once one's virginity has been (un)ceremoniously lost. In an ideal world, the uninitiated virgin would be prepared, unhurried, only slightly apprehensive and - naturally - totally in love. However, there are always some who seem to want to get it over with as quickly as possible. After all, sex isn't something you can plan right down to the very last detail, especially when you don't really have the first idea what the hell it's all about. So the first time might be amazing, or it may well put you off forever.

*Scenario One*: slight flutter of nervous excitement, best new underwear, candlelight and chilled wine, freshly-washed and scented body which pulses with desire, soft background music, clean satin sheets, mutually-agreed choice of contraception, a gorgeous, beautiful partner who knows how to use their tongue, prolonged foreplay, earth-shattering, synchronised orgasms, post-coital affection and cerebral chat; no regrets.

*Scenario Two*: Blind drunk and desperate, saggy, week-old undies, tepid beer and a slight feeling of nausea, the stench of stale perspiration and bad breath, crumpled, stained sheets on a knackered old bed, unappealing partner who exacerbates your impending need to throw up and whose name you keep forgetting, the phrases like "Is it in yet?" and "Was that it?", no foreplay, no contraception, hazy recollection of it the next morning. Plenty of regrets.

# first orgasm

There seems to be a fairly decisive split between male and female experiences of the first orgasm. And, contrary to popular belief, it might just be the women who have the more natural approach. The orgasm, after all, is the quintessential sexual experience - the out-of-body thrill that signifies the pinnacle of mutual intimacy. It's something which deserves to be strived towards, laboured at, earnt. Like any reward, or extraordinary experience, its qualities should be enhanced through chance achievement or earnest nurturing.

All well and good, but most lads learn at thirteen to knock one off over their Dad's playmates calendar and they carry on doing so every morning and evening for the next four or five years. This teaches them a very different lesson about the orgasm: how to do it quickly, quietly and alone so that no one catches you.

Thus, the inevitable clumsiness and embarrassment when it finally comes to sex - a couple of minutes, the faintest of grunts and a hasty roll away from that 'other person' that was there at the time. Thus, also the marvel when (and if) the man is lucky enough to witness his partner orgasm: its ecstatic power and intensity, wrestled into being through love and patience. What man wouldn't swap a couple of years leafing through sticky pornos for just a moment of that kind of bliss?

# the first car

Previously you relied on reluctant family members to deliver you to essential social functions. "I'm not a bloody taxi," lamented your father. Indeed, he was something far better: unlike taxis he never charged, he always found your house in the dark and didn't rabbit on about debauched exploits with female passengers. He was, in fact, your *chauffeur*.

Clutching your new car keys, you realise you are on the verge of youth's final rite of passage. A first real show of independence. You are free to roam the world beyond your home. Free to career down country lanes, girlfriend by your side, cares breezing away. Free to travel wherever the road takes you.

Or at least that's how it first seems. But, you soon realise, that, though you could go anywhere, you won't. You won't because, after tax, MOT, exorbitant insurance and the (comparatively cheap) cost of the 1974 Escort of your choice, you are left with barely enough cash for a half tank of petrol. To top it all, the old banger has probably been so poorly maintained you gamble with your life every time you step on the brakes. Two cars welded together do not, alas, represent good value for money.

Should the car actually go from A to B, you will find that 'B' is rarely further than the local pub. It's now *your* job to transport close friends and tenuous acquaintances to and from it every night. It is your begrudging annoyance to let everyone else 'out at the lights', and seek a parking space alone. Your job to be 'responsible' for the rest of the night. You have become your dad. *You* are now the chauffeur.

In years to come you will look back on your first car with fondness; the same kind of fondness you feel for a socially inept relative you no longer visit. But for now, as the only sober person in the pub, you think of your father supping a whiskey in the comfort of his armchair, safe in the knowledge that *his* chauffeur days are over.

# first term at university

For a boring few, university is all about academia, higher education and free access to enormous libraries. For the rest it's about defining yourself as a human being. Or, to be more precise, *re-defining* yourself. Back home everybody knows you. They've watched you grow up. People look at you and still see the kid who nearly drowned in her primary school swimming gala, who wet her knickers at the back of the school bus at twelve and who dated Barry 'the boil' Hargreaves for three years.

University, then, provides an opportunity to break from the torment of your past. You suddenly have freedom: to do whatever and *be* whoever you want.

Unfortunately this sudden freedom proves overwhelming for most first year students and you find yourself unable to achieve individuality that even approaches wet panties on school buses. Instead you become defined in herds: rammed into late night clubs, stuck in drinking games, throwing up on buses, waking in strange beds, arriving late for classes and suffering from hangovers.

It is strange that what starts as a desire for personal re-definition manifests itself in communal hedonism. Strange also that, by the end of the first term, you are happy to have your parents pick you up. It's almost pride you feel as your Dad enters the hall of residence in his best argyle cardigan and your Mum starts complaining loudly that you've lost too much weight. Pride in the past that sets you apart from countless identical parties. Pride in the two people who can best define you away from the pack. And, perhaps most importantly, pride in the fact that you feel this way at all.

The most important part of growing up is appreciating where you've come from and nothing inspires appreciation so much as the first time you move away from home.

# the first credit card

It is a popular misconception that students have to struggle financially. It *is* true that most students have no money, but that is not to say that they were always penniless. Indeed, they start their college years with a plethora of financial institutions to which they can turn. University banks actively recommend £9000 overdrafts to cover alcohol expenses. Student loan companies offer the cheapest interest rates and longest periods of deferment you're ever likely to find. But even the thousands that can be gleaned from these loans are quickly spent on student essentials: a new hi-fi, a second-hand BMW, a dozen or so romantic meals for you and your girlfriend.

Sadly, student loans have limits - even if the students themselves don't.

It's at this stage in the game (around the fourth week of the first term) that hunger sets in. Empty larders now inspire many students to take a more active role in their finances ... In their thousands they fill out credit card application forms.

After many days of sobriety and snacking on ketchup sandwiches, the card arrives and with it the prospect at last of some good food. Many take this opportunity to convince themselves that they must make amends and make their money go further. But the first shopping receipts often read the same: one Versace jumper, designer sunglasses, a Hugo Boss overcoat, a games console, Nike gym shoes, a video player, a selection of new CDs, a lava lamp, an Indian wall-hanging, a bottle of Jack Daniels, a crate of beer and a couple of microwave curries for the rest of the week.

This kind of mistake is made only once. Most students are consequently blacklisted well into their thirties.

# first proper job

As a young adult you can now look back and see that your night shifts on the Donut kiosk did not really constitute a 'proper job'. £9.80 an hour for sitting in a mobile cupboard! It was clear even then that society had groomed you for a better role.

The ten interviews you passed to get into Cuthbert, Carmichael and Shaw were a far cry from 'How old are you?' - the kiosk owner's only concern. Jeffrey Carmichael himself had sat and watched as his partners unpicked your mind and character. And you must have impressed them with that brave surmise on South Vietnamese tax law, because they decided in your favour.

You know you will need to impress your clients from day one, so you invest in a tailored suit, gold cufflinks, Armani shirt and new brogues. The night before, you briefly revise European immigration, recognising it as a personal weakness and convinced it'll crop up on your first day.

By 9.30 the following morning Jackie from personnel is showing you to your desk. It's next to the photocopier. Just in front of the coffee machine. Quite close to the stationery cupboard. You observe, with pride, your *own* phone on the desk. It rings and Jackie motions you to answer it...

...Four hundred similar internal calls later and your hands are sore, from carrying hot drinks around the office. You'd hoped by now Mr Carmichael would have praised you for your knowledge of Hungarian exchange rates, not for bringing him Boasters instead of Digestives. But it's early days. In fact, Jackie said if you worked hard, by July you'd move up to filing.

That night your aching body sleeps well. Your blissful dreams are all of immigration and European business. And, for one night, Utopia is a life on the continent in your *own* mobile donut kiosk.

# first love

We are all selfish, never more so than during our youth, when life is all about acquisition. Education, independence, money, praise, popularity - all essential ingredients to a well-rounded adult, not so much won as demanded by the ambitious teenager.

However, many experiences of youth are tinged with a quality quite different to this unrelenting self-service. The quiet tears your mother cried when your father fell ill, the pink sunset over Tuscan churches you finally witnessed on that first holiday alone. There was a beauty and detachment to those moments that spoke of a deeper quality to life. And, though fleeting, you feel deficient without its serenity and peace.

You never quite learn the measure of this quality until you fall in love. And still you may never be able to precisely define what has actually happened to you. Suffice to say, one day you come across someone whose very smile, speech and manner affect you as those moments did. And you are drawn out of yourself.

The first love is a mixture of bliss and vulnerability. That feeling of beauty, which had previously existed in fleeting moments, can now last days in another person's company. But like an addiction, you want to drown in this emotion - your happiness now reliant on the actions and reactions of that other person.

You grow in two ways: inspired by the beauty of unity, you may find yourself making natural emotional bonds with the world around you. But you also open yourself up to a new pain, since that other person's behaviour can easily affect your happiness. This makes you doubly aware of the effect of everyday words and actions - for even when you hurt your lover, you inevitably find their pain is yours.

The first love helps refine your perception of the world. Love that shows you the power of altruism. Love that reverses the focus of your entire life. Milestones don't come any more profound than this, which is why no one ever forgets, or ever stops loving, the one they loved first.

# first marriage

The soft yellow light filters through the curtains. You are awake before her. Her head is turned towards you and she breathes slowly and easily. You raise your head a little on one elbow. She is even more beautiful than she had been the morning before, when you turned to see her entering the church, the light glowing from beneath her skin. She came to you up the aisle, both shy and bold, her eyes on you only. Her father on her arm, stiff and slightly theatrical, her mother, small and vital. As she came closer the cold air of the church gave way to the gentle breath of spring and your heart opened.

And now, in the quiet of the morning, you notice a vulnerability and innocence in the woman that has chosen to be with you, a trusting serenity that encourages your love. You have made your vows to protect this beauty and the responsibility fills you with gratitude and humility. The swell and curve of her body are just imaginable under the duvet ("It's all going south" she would joke). But you know that this is what you have been charged to protect - by her, by those who live by her and now by God. You see in her naked form the canvas on which you will trace the map of your love and your losses, your passion, your fights and your persistence. The responsibility is awesome and yet your heart is stronger than ever.

Her face reflects the stillness of her soul. She stirs and her eyes half open as she looks at you. You know she sees the same as you do. Your hearts open once again.

# first house

Buying a house is probably one of the most stressful, and certainly the most expensive of life's firsts. You'll think you've saved up enough cash to buy a small country by the time you start looking in earnest for your own place. But nothing prepares you for the shock of your entire life savings bled dry before you've even ordered the removals van.

You have to enlist the professional help of a snide estate agent and a bored and insanely overpaid solicitor who will send you endless bills and evade your phone calls. Weekends are now reserved for fighting your way through Ikea and flicking through Argos catalogues. You will be comparing and contrasting mortgages and the relative benefits of fixed, variable and capped rates with such fanatical regularity that most of your friends will disown you. You have to buy all the things you promised yourself you would never own: an ironing board, a clothes airer, a sandwich toaster, a vacuum cleaner, a teapot. Meanwhile, other people keep buying you storage jars and Tupperware containers until you've run out of ideas of what to keep in them.

Finally, after months of exhaustion and expense, you are handed the keys to your home. You sit on the summit of your mountain of boxes and look around at bare walls - the empty space that is now officially yours. You wonder: was it worth it?

Don't forget you still have the unpacking, assembling, painting, decorating, cleaning, sorting and stocking to look forward to. And of course, the house-warming party - because after all this effort, it's tradition to let your friends puke up on the new carpets.

# first baby

Anyone with an ounce of rational reasoning would be forgiven for assuming that this very special and very painful first event should really be the first and only of its kind. If you're the unfortunate one who's just pushed the little darling out, you may want to get your feet out of the stirrups, pledge a lifelong vow of chastity, forget about your stretchmarks, episiotomy scars and leaking nipples, curl up in a quiet room on your own and fall asleep for a million years. But for many mothers those nine weighty months before the inevitable genital-stretching conclusion are willingly - even joyously - repeated as many as five or six times.

The birth of the first baby is, without doubt, the most overwhelmingly life-affirming experience anyone will ever go through. Until this moment, most will have lived their lives taking from the world as best they could, 'making themselves', amassing, plundering, climbing. But, when your life engenders another, the direction of your world reverses. The first child is *physical* proof that you cannot live for yourself and consequently you learn to cherish life as a universal gift, not just something *you* happen to have.

Of course, this kind of thinking doesn't make parenting any easier, so it's best to make the most of your child whilst it still looks adorably cute. It won't be long before it's running amok, destroying and terrorising its environment in equal measure. And that's long before you get to the delightful teenage years.

# the first wrinkle

The sight of the first wrinkle generates a nightmare of masochistic activity from which all pleasure is absent. The trouble is, the first wrinkle inexorably draws the gaze to the next, and the next. You move towards the light, peering into the bathroom mirror. My God! Your eyes are surrounded! Your face is under attack! What about the rest of you? You bound upstairs and strip off. And there, hideous to behold, is the truth. You not only have a wrinkle or three on your face, you are developing little folds at the base of your bum. Quick, quick, the gym! You must enrol in the gym!

You always swore you wouldn't, but needs must when the wrinkles drive. You cut down a pair of old leggings and borrow someone's sweatshirt. Damned if you're going to buy any of that special gear. And off you go.

Humiliation greets you. You can't take your eyes off those skinny women with thonged leotards cutting into their buttocks. What on earth does it do to their fannies? And bones. They're all bones. You can see the outline of each carefully starved pelvis. And they've got ribs. No breasts though, ha ha! You do a frantic warm up on the bicycle. Ten minutes slaughter and only twenty nine calories! It can't be true. Hurling yourself at a series of machines you just about complete the circuit and wind up, red and sweaty, on the treadmill. Glancing up at the wall-to-wall mirror, hoping for some little sign of improvement, what should you see scowling back at you, but the unmistakable jowls of your mother. That's when you know for sure. After the first wrinkle, it's downhill all the way.

# first realization your parents were right

The words spew from your mouth as if you'd been rehearsing them for years: "Because this is MY house! And as long as you live in this house and eat MY food, use MY telephone and waste MY electricity you will obey MY rules!" They hang in a horrified silence - words you had vowed you would never say to your children. Attitudes of dominance based on economic control instead of emotional reason. Your mother had spoken right from your own mouth. And what's horrifying is it wasn't all that hard to do.

You behold your child, decorated with tattoos and piercings, standing arms crossed before you, her eyes rolling in disgust towards the ceiling as if dismissing a drunk at the train station. Your fears and lack of parental control had pushed you over the edge. It was the first time you had spoken those words - a first invocation of your mother's belief in 'discipline through intimidation'. It was also the first time you felt completely justified in doing so.

There comes a time in every parent's life when their unconditional giving reaches a dead end. When they ask their able-bodied teens for a smidgen of compliance and a dollop of respect for serving as their twenty four hour cash machine, taxi driver and catering service. You bask in the triumph for a full five seconds.

"Right," you say, "That was a ludicrous comment. Here's the deal I want you home by midnight because I am afraid you will be killed on the street after that. Could you humour me for two more years and spare me the heart attack and early grave that your lifestyle is leading me to?"

Your child says she'll try. That's also a first.

# first bereavement

Most of us are so reliant on those closest to us it is difficult to accept that our relationships are transient. But, surely, as each day passes, the lifespan of every bond decreases. Eventually, whether sooner or later, something has to give. It's the one thing in life you can be absolutely certain of.

There are times of course, even in the happiest of relationships, when murder seems a not unattractive proposition, but by and large, we're too busy being alive to think of dying.

It's only when the first tell-tale signs of mortality mock you from the bathroom mirror, and words previously unused begin to pepper your conversation - words like 'prostate' and 'Saga holidays', that you begin to consider that remote and incomprehensible possibility.

Then one day, maybe without warning, maybe after a period of endless exhaustion, you find yourself gazing in disbelief at the still body of the one you loved through good times and bad, for all those years. Guilt follows swiftly. Unspoken words of love and contrition make a shipwreck of your nights. "Why did I do that? Did I tell you I loved you? How can I thank you now? Forgive me." You become cocooned in silence because other people are too embarrassed to greet you in the street, to speak the name you long to hear. You talk wildly into the darkness. "Where are you? Why did you leave me? And who am I, now that you are gone?" You move into a vast empty space that has no boundaries, lost, carrying your grief like a physical pain. Until one morning, two years, three years, four years later, you wake up and notice, as if for the first time, a faint colour in the sky.

# first realization your children are adults

You are negotiating the roundabout on a chilly autumn morning when a car swerves into your lane. You hit the horn and simultaneously fling a protective arm wildly across to your left as you brake. Your daughter in the passenger seat takes hold of your arm and gently places it back into your lap. "Mother I am twenty one, six inches taller than you, outweigh you by forty pounds and I already have a seat belt on. What did you think your arm would protect me from?"

"I am sorry," you protest, "I am afflicted with the 'mother's arm'. I developed it before seat belts and child seats when you were three-years-old." You look down at your comparatively puny arm. It doesn't seem to recognize the fact that your child has been replaced by a fully-grown woman. In fact, it's the first time you realize that the child isn't coming back. Your arm isn't the only thing slow on the uptake.

But it's hard - whenever you see her, you still have her pet name on the tip of your tongue, 'Bouncer'. You have learned long ago not to humiliate her with that name, but she will always be your little Bouncer even when you are ninety and she is sixty and you are half her size. You look at her and hear yourself say - Bouncer, Bouncer, Bouncer. She thinks the name is dead and gone, but you're saving it to tell her children so they can torture her with it when you're gone.

This realization is the start. When children stop asking for money, when you have holidays at their house and can graciously eat the tofu turkey for Christmas, when you accept that their choice of a life partner or no partner is, well, their choice. When you can see them as they were and as they are, well, I guess that's when you know you're both grown-ups.

# first day of retirement

Something at the backdoor of your dream says, '6.00am6.00am6.00am6.00am6.00am'. You fumble for the light and slowly awake. Faceless anxieties are crystallising in the still, cold air. You lie there for a minute as consciousness returns.

"You don't have to do this any more!" "You don't have to do this ever again!" "Why should I worry?" "They can paddle their own canoe." You get up anyway and put on walking boots and a green shirt (You don't do ties anymore). Your wife asks what the hell you are doing. "See you in an hour," you reply.

You walk down the lane and over the fields to where the train runs over an embankment.

The early mist lies still over the lake. The yellow morning reaches up.

Suddenly, the 7.08 to London. They stare blankly from the windows. You consider a rude gesture but pity and residual politeness hold you back. Instead you watch quietly and wave goodbye.

It's all gone now.

The parting birds turn low over the water as their instincts gather them on. The weak rising sun is at your back as you come down the path to where your wife is starting breakfast.

The pub up the road does full English breakfast and toast and tea for your wife ("We can't do this every day do you want a coronary?") It's good to celebrate, to put down a marker. That's your starting block. But it's cross-country now. There are no lane markings. Noone at your shoulder, no pounding feet behind.

You look out of the window. The mist is lifting. Yes, it's Autumn. But your wife says,

"This is the first Monday of the Future!"

# first grandchild

Ever wondered why parents get so excited about having grandkids? With twenty odd years of un-rewarded service behind them and the screams of teenage abuse still ringing in their ears, it's a remarkably forgiving attitude. Why aren't there more elderly ladies in the streets bashing kids with walking sticks and letting their terriers off the leash whenever they walk past a primary school? In general, grandchildren are thought to be a blessing - either because early senility has brought with it gross forgetfulness, or because kids carry a significance beyond sewage production, projectile vomiting and red-faced bawling.

Perhaps this significance lies in the fact that the first grandchild completes an entire cycle of life. A cycle of firsts. With its arrival, the grandparent starts again - with no less circumstantial wonder and excitement than before - but this time with an understanding that stems from having already completed the course once. And where their children will throw themselves into parenting with all the characteristic vigour of the first-timer, they themselves will know when to hold back - when to charge at an obstacle and when to walk around it.

Maybe this is why so many grandparents can be found backhanding money, sweets and irreverent advice to their young charges. It's not to sabotage their own children's hard work, but to put propriety aside for a moment and spread a little happiness. When you grapple with life's problems, it's easy to forget to be happy. No more so than during parenthood. But, having lapped everyone else, grandparents can apply perspective to the lives around them. They know whether to lose sleep over a playground fight or save their worry for the inevitable tragedies that some days will bring their young family.

Hence the £20 notes hidden in Mars Bar wrappers, the candid stories and the seven thousand calorie diet every grandchild enjoys at their grandparents' house. It's called having fun and maybe it's universally felt that, first time around, there wasn't quite enough of it.